The World of Composers

Beethoven

Greta Cencetti

PETER BEDRICK BOOKS

McGraw-Hill
Children's Publishing
A Division of The **McGraw-Hill** Companies

This edition published in the United States in 2002 by
Peter Bedrick Books, an imprint of
McGraw-Hill Children's Publishing,
A Division of The McGraw-Hill Companies
8787 Orion Place
Columbus, Ohio 43240

www.MHkids.com

ISBN 1-58845-468-1

Library of Congress Cataloging-in-Publication Data

Cencetti, Greta.
Beethoven / Greta Cencetti.
p. cm. -- (The world of composers)
Summary: A simple survey of the life of the German composer who showed
his musical talents from an early age.
ISBN 1-58845-468-1
1. Beethoven, Ludwig van, 1770-1827--Juvenile literature. 2. Composers—
Austria—Vienna—Biography—Juvenile literature. [1. Beethoven, Ludwig van,
1770-1827. 2. Composers.] I. Title. II. Series.

ML3930.B4 C46 2002
780'.92--dc21
[B]
2001052415

© 2002 Ta Chien Publishing Co., Ltd.
© 2002 Studio Mouse

10 9 8 7 6 5 4 3 2 1 CHRT 06 05 04 03 02

Printed in China.

The World of Composers

Beethoven

Greta Cencetti

PETER BEDRICK BOOKS

Contents

Chapter		Page
1	Beethoven's Birthplace	7
2	The Young Musician	15
3	Beethoven's Career Begins	17
4	Vienna	19
5	Court Musician	23
6	Success	27
7	Beethoven's Secret	29
8	A Life of Loneliness	30
9	Beethoven's Greatest Works	35
10	A Turning Point in Musical History	37
11	Beethoven's Last Days	38
	Introduction to the Harpsichord	40

Chapter 1
Beethoven's Birthplace

Over two hundred years ago, the Beethoven (pronounced BAY-toh-vuhn) family lived in the city of Bonn, in Prussia (present-day Germany).

Records show that Ludwig van Beethoven was baptized on December 17, 1770. His parents were Johann and Maria Magdalena van Beethoven. Ludwig was named after his grandfather, who was a great musician.

During Beethoven's time, Bonn was under the rule of a powerful prince called the Prince Elector. Many nobles, ladies, attendants, artists, and musicians lived in the Prince Elector's palace. Beethoven's grandfather was among them. He served as the court musician and entertained the nobles with music and song.

Beethoven's grandfather became famous because he was the Prince Elector's favorite musician. Young Beethoven and his grandfather would often walk through the palace gardens. During their walks, Beethoven's grandfather would tell him that someday, he too, would be playing music for the royal families.

When Beethoven was around six years old, his father began to give him violin and harpsichord lessons. The young boy showed great promise in music even at this early age.

Chapter 2
The Young Musician

At the age of eight, Beethoven's father arranged for him to perform in public for the feudal prince of Cologne, who ruled in that city, near Bonn.

The feudal prince of Cologne was so impressed by young Ludwig's talents that he wrote to the Prince Elector, telling him that the young boy was a musical genius. The Prince Elector, in turn, offered young Beethoven the chance to learn music from Christian Gottlob Neefe, thought to be the best musician in Bonn. Neefe was the court organist, and Beethoven served as his assistant.

Beethoven played the violin and the harpsichord, but the moving sounds of the organ were especially inspiring to him. Soon, he was playing the organ as well. Beethoven displayed so much ability that the Prince Elector offered him the job of church organist.

Beethoven's great talent and ability did not go unnoticed in Bonn. By the age of 12, he was composing new pieces for concerts. Beethoven loved nature. The sounds of a thunderstorm and a raging river inspired him to write powerful music. His first published works were for the clavier (an early keyboard instrument), based on a march by composer Ernst Christoph Dressler.

Chapter 3
Beethoven's Career Begins

*I*n 1784, the Prince Elector died. A man named Joseph Franz Maximilian Lobkowitz became the new prince. Prince Lobkowitz was determined to turn the city of Bonn into a place rich in art and culture. He invited artists and scholars to stay in his palace. After hearing of Beethoven's talent, the prince appointed him the organist of his private chapel. This was the first time Beethoven received payment for performing music.

Chapter 4
Vienna

*I*n the years that followed, Beethoven helped support his family with the money he earned performing. When he turned 17, Prince Lobkowitz offered to send him to Vienna to continue his studies in music. Vienna was home to all the great musicians of Europe. During Beethoven's time, it was a city where the sound of music could be heard from nearly every street and square.

In 1787, Beethoven packed his clothes and his compositions. He set off by horse and coach to visit Vienna.

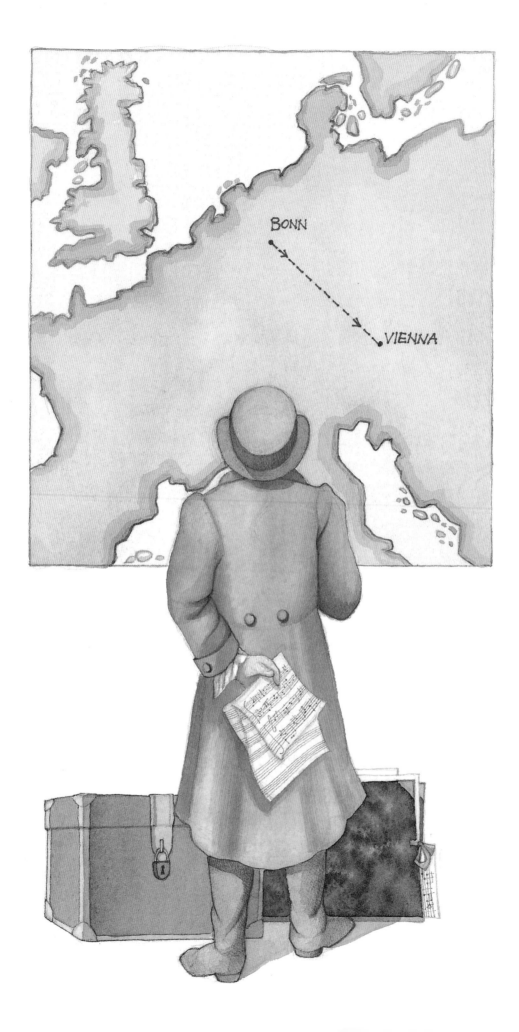

Shortly after his arrival in Vienna, Beethoven received news that his mother was seriously ill. He returned to Bonn, but sadly his mother died of tuberculosis a short time later. After his mother's death, Beethoven began playing viola in the court orchestra in Bonn, a job he held for four years.

Prince Waldstein, a music lover who was extremely impressed by Beethoven's music, talked him into returning to Vienna. The prince knew Beethoven would be successful there.

Chapter 5
Court Musician

With the help of Prince Waldstein and his connections, Beethoven was welcomed to Vienna by many of the city's leading nobles. He stayed at the home of Prince Lichnowksy, who, along with his wife Princess Christiane, became Beethoven's leading supporters.

Beethoven had opportunities to display his talent at the palaces and estates of the nobles. A Hungarian man named Nikolaus Zmeskall von Domanovecz was another great supporter of Beethoven's, and he promoted performances of Beethoven's music.

Chapter 6
Success

*B*eethoven played his music in the homes of nobles and was so well-received that many of them asked him to teach music to their children. Beethoven had numerous works published, and his name soon spread throughout Europe. He was quickly becoming a highly respected composer.

Beethoven was the master of the piano, the musical instrument that had replaced the harpsichord. The range of sounds that could be produced by playing the piano was particularly suited to Beethoven's powerful, yet sensitive touch.

Chapter 7
Beethoven's Secret

*I*n 1795, when the musician was only 25, tragedy struck. Beethoven heard a strange buzzing sound in his ears. The sound grew and grew until a few years later, he lost his hearing completely.

Beethoven kept his deafness a secret for several years. He had not given up hope that the doctors could do something for him. He also feared that his deafness would have a profound effect on both his professional and social life.

Finally, he wrote letters to two of his closest friends and told them about his secret. A doctor made a hearing aid for Beethoven with the hope it would help him. The device resembled a horn. Its small end was to be placed in the ear, and the other end of the horn had a wide opening to draw sound in. Unfortunately, it did not help. Beethoven would never hear again.

Chapter 8
A Life of Loneliness

Perhaps because of his deafness, Beethoven's personality changed. He developed a terrible temper, and, as a result, he lost many of his friends.

In Vienna, he moved 13 times. Badly depressed, he quarreled with friends, even those who had helped, encouraged, and supported him when he first moved to Vienna.

Although Beethoven was deaf, he did not stop composing. A group of nobles gathered together to support Beethoven financially so that he could continue to write music. Many music lovers feel that Beethoven's compositions grew more passionate and beautiful after he became deaf.

It is said that the people of Vienna would often see Beethoven walking around the city in a dark overcoat. He carried a notebook in his pocket so that he could write music down as ideas came to him. As time passed, Beethoven stayed home more and more. He spent whole days at his piano composing and performing. People who missed his performances would gather at the half-opened door of his piano room. From there, they could hear the sounds of his beautiful music and new compositions.

Chapter 9

Beethoven's Greatest Works

*T*wo of Beethoven's best-known works were inspired by events in his life. *Moonlight Sonata* was inspired by his relationship with the Countess Giulietta Guicciardi. Giulietta was the daughter of a duke, and she and Beethoven were in love. She married a count, though, in keeping with her noble class. Beethoven's loss of Giulietta inspired him to compose the glorious *Moonlight Sonata* and dedicate it to her.

Beethoven's *Symphony No. 3* premiered in 1805. This symphony was originally nicknamed *Bonaparte*, in tribute to the young hero of revolutionary France, Napoleon Bonaparte. But Beethoven became angry when he found out that Bonaparte crowned himself emperor of the French in 1804. He then changed the nickname of the symphony to the *Eroica* (heroic) *Symphony*, and dedicated it to Prince Lobkowitz.

Chapter 10
A Turning Point in Musical History

*I*n 1815, Beethoven's younger brother died, leaving behind his young son, Karl. Beethoven was very fond of the boy and became his guardian. When Karl reached school age, he attended a boarding school. Once his schooling was over, he joined the army, leaving Beethoven alone again.

In 1824, Beethoven completed his last great work, *Symphony No. 9*. In this symphony, Beethoven introduced a choral ending based on a well-known German poem, "Ode to Joy." This symphony became the first ever to combine the orchestra with a chorus of singers. It displayed Beethoven's creativity and imagination, and it is still popular today.

In that same year, with the encouragement of friends, Beethoven conducted a concert. During the performance, with his back to the audience, Beethoven was completely unaware of the thunderous applause. It is said that one of the lead singers pulled him by the sleeve and pointed to the audience. Beethoven bowed to the audience, accepting the appreciation.

Chapter 11
Beethoven's Last Days

*I*n the winter of 1826, Beethoven returned to Vienna from the countryside. He made the journey in an open carriage in extremely cold, harsh weather.

After Beethoven arrived home, he developed a raging fever. Although a doctor treated him, Beethoven's illness did not improve. He was confined to bed for months. His friends sent gifts to comfort him.

Ludwig van Beethoven died on March 26, 1827. Thousands of people gathered in the square near his home to attend his funeral. Beethoven spent much of his life in his own lonely world, but he gave the rest of the world beautiful music filled with passion and power.

Introduction to the Harpsichord

The harpsichord is one of the first instruments that Beethoven learned to play. The harpsichord is a keyboard instrument that was popular from the sixteenth through the eighteenth centuries. It preceded the piano, which was not invented until the early eighteenth century.

The harpsichord was used actively throughout the eighteenth century for solo music, as part of small music ensembles, and as an orchestra instrument. By 1810, the harpsichord was no longer used, but it became popular again in the twentieth century.

The strings contained inside the body of the harpsichord are plucked as the performer's fingers strike the keys. In contrast, the strings inside a piano are struck by hammers.

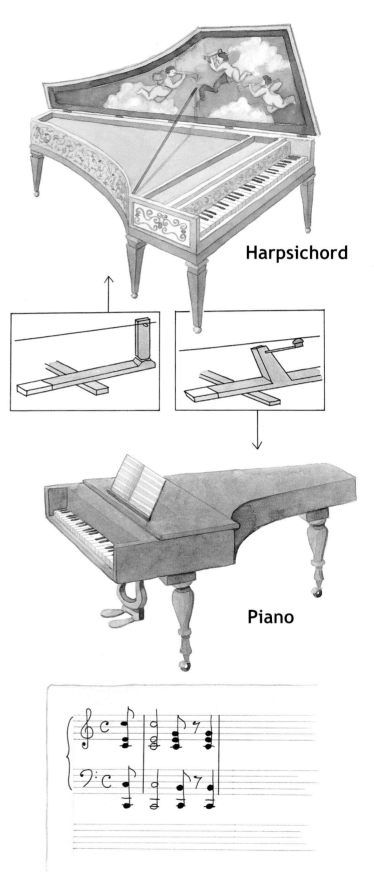

Harpsichord

Piano